LOVE IN A THIRSTY LAND

Alan Glass

BROADWAY PLAY PUBLISHING INC
New York
www.broadwayplaypublishing.com
info@broadwayplaypublishing.com

Cover image by Hy Varon
First printing July 2011
I S B N: 978-0-88145-487-1
Book design: Marie Donovan
Page make-up: Adobe Indesign
Typeface: Palatino
Printed and bound in the U S A

LOVE IN A THIRSTY LAND opened on 19 February 2000, presented by the Jewish Repertory Theater (Ran Avni, Artstic Director), New York City. The cast and creative contributors were:

GEORGE STEPHENSON .... David Hess
PESACH RUBENSTEIN .... David Julian Hirsh
SARA ALEXANDER ....Susan May Pratt
LEAH SKLARSKY.. Suzanne Toren
ISAAC SHMULWITZ... Lee Beltzer

Director..Robert Kalfin
Sets..Mark Nayden
Costumes.. Gail Cooper-Hecht
Lighting...Chris Dallos
Sound design...Margaret Pine
Fight choreography .... B H Barry
Production stage manager ....D C Rosenberg
Assistant stage manager .... Peggy R Samuels
Assistant director......................................Cailin Heffernan
Casting.. Irene Stockton
Advisor............................. Rabbi Abraham Eckstein, PhD

Production by arrangement with Mary Ellen Ashley and Shar Visions Productions

CHARACTERS & SETTING

Isaac Shmulwitz
Theodore Stephenson, *35-55*
Leah Sklarsky, *40s*
Pesach Rubenstein, *21*
Sara Alexander, *19*

Manhattan, Brooklyn

All scenes in 1874 except those denoted 1875

Sets/scenery: when necessary, simple props will serve to convey a scene setting. Leg shackles, a bed, a hat form, a park bench, door frame, laundry, and picnic baskets are examples.

SCENES

ACT ONE
1. Jail
2. Bedroom
3. Parlor
4. Laundry room
5. Parlor
6. River's Edge
7. Bedroom

ACT TWO
1. Jail
2. Field
3. Parlor
4. Laundry
5. Jail
6. Field
7. Courtroom

for Babette, who lives in memory

ACT ONE

Scene One

(1875. Jailhouse. STEPHENSON *at window. Outside rowdy singing, "Rubenstein, Rubenstein, you'll look fine swinging on the hangman's line. "Hang the Jew!" etc.* STEPHENSON *looks out window, turns away angrily.* LEAH *arrives.)*

STEPHENSON: Mrs Sklarsky.

LEAH: Mister Stephenson. *(Looks around)* Where is he?

STEPHENSON: *(Points)* In his cell.

LEAH: He's sick again?

STEPHENSON: He's not well. But that's not why he asked you to come.

*(*LEAH *puzzled)*

STEPHENSON: It has something to do with...religion. Regretfully, he doesn't let me in on his secrets.

*(*LEAH *and* STEPHENSON *move toward cell.)*

STEPHENSON: He calls me "Brass buttons?" What's he talking about?

LEAH: We called the Czar's police the Brass Buttons.

STEPHENSON: I'm not the police!! Doesn't he know I'm on his side?

LEAH: I told him who you were. How famous you were.

(*Louder crowd noise, "Hang the Christ killer!"* LEAH *looks, she's scared.*)

STEPHENSON: Drunks. They're here every time somebody's tried for murder. Now—they have their first Hebrew! (*Holds up paper*) It's these damn newspapers!

LEAH: (*Pointing to headline*) Ridiculous. My nephew shouldn't even be here!

STEPHENSON: As you know, the grand jury disagreed.

LEAH: The grandson of a great rabbi, a boy who prays to the Almighty three times a day? He's an innocent boy!

STEPHENSON: All my clients are innocent. That's why they engage me.

LEAH: (*Upset*) You don't understand—he *is* innocent! (*Walking to cell*)

STEPHENSON: Let him tell me! Tell me *something*. I didn't take this case, at considerable financial sacrifice, to lose!

(LEAH *and* STEPHENSON *arrive at cell.* PESACH, *wearing hat—always—is behind bars.*)

LEAH: Pesach! Look at you!

(PESACH *coughs.*)

LEAH: He was very sick once. A terrible cough and fever.

STEPHENSON: Rubenstein, do you want me to get a doctor?

PESACH: No. No doctor. I said before.

LEAH: They said you're not eating! (*Takes food from bag*) I have some bread, herring. Kosher food!

(PESACH *waves food away.*)

LEAH: Eat! You have to eat to live.

PESACH: Kosher food's not why I asked you here, Leah.
(Takes out prayer shawl)

LEAH: What are you doing?! Time for morning prayer
is over!

PESACH: Take it. Have Uncle Laibl dispose of it
properly.

LEAH: What? What are you talking about?

PESACH: *(Attempts to hand over prayer shawl)* It's a sin to
leave this here rotting in this stinking wet cell. Tell him
bury it, like you bury a dead loved one.

LEAH: You have to say the prayers with those!

PESACH: I stopped saying the prayers. *(Again tries to
hand over shawl)*

LEAH: What are you doing?!!

PESACH: Take it. All of it.

LEAH: I will not!! You need prayer things.

PESACH: *(Removing fringed vest from under shirt)* Take
this, too!

LEAH: Stop! Don't take it off! Think of the commands of
God.

PESACH: I want to *stop* thinking about the commands of
God. You have to help me. You and Uncle Laibl.

LEAH: I will not! You're mourning for her, that's all.

PESACH: *(Pointing to prayer artifacts)* I don't want them
here. I'm separating myself from God.

LEAH: "Separating Yourself From God"!! The grandson
of five generations of rabbis—and you say a thing like
that!

(PESACH *looks away.*)

LEAH: God will help you, Pesach. It is written: "Men who sit in darkness, bound in iron...cry out to the Lord, and God delivers them from their distress."

PESACH: Look around Leah. Where is the light of God!

LEAH: *(Holds up prayer articles) These* are the light of God.

PESACH: Once they were. No more!

STEPHENSON: Mrs Sklarsky, do what your nephew asks, please. Take them away.

LEAH: I will not.

STEPHENSON: Bring them back later, if he wants them.

LEAH: Separating himself from God!! What kind of thing is that to say!

STEPHENSON: *(His forbearance fading)* The most important thing right now—for the sake of this trial—is uncovering more about his relationship with that girl!

PESACH: *(Angry, coughs, sputters)* She is not "that girl!"

LEAH: Pesach! Be respectful! He's your lawyer. He usually charges more than any of them!

STEPHENSON: *(To* LEAH, *pointing to prayer items)* Away with those things immediately, please!!

*(*LEAH *gathers them up reluctantly.)*

STEPHENSON: Thank you. *(He gestures for her to leave.)* Rubenstein! Start again! Sara Alexander! The dead girl. Tell me about her.

*(*PESACH *coughs,* LEAH *turns.)*

LEAH: When he was sick, that's when he met her. That was my fault.

STEPHENSON: Rubenstein, you were sick and coughing, I understand.

PESACH: *(Weak laugh)* Sara took my breath away! *(Wan smile, coughs)* I'm tired. I don't want to talk!

STEPHENSON: Do I have to remind you, your trial starts in less than a week.

PESACH: Guard! Guard!!

LEAH: *(Moving off, stops)* Pesach, we gave all our savings to hire this man. Cousin Yaacov sold his horse and wagon.

PESACH: Give the money back, Mister Stephenson. These are poor people.

LEAH: *(Exiting slowly)* This lawyer—all of his clients are alive! Don't forget that.

PESACH: I don't need him. *(He coughs again.)*

LEAH: Not helping save your life, Pesach, is the same as the sin of hastening your death.

STEPHENSON: Do you hear that, Mr. Rubenstein?

LEAH: Only the Almighty who gave you breath can decide when to take it away!

STEPHENSON: *(Points to door, turns to PESACH)* Those sacred things—see your aunt is removing them. Now, you tell me about Sara Alexander.

LEAH: *(At door)* Pesach, please! People call him a miracle lawyer! *(Exits)*

PESACH: *(To STEPHENSON)* I don't need miracles.

STEPHENSON: What did you say to Sara—Sara to you—when you first met her? *(Angry at no response)* I did what you wanted! I got those religious objects out of here. Now—it's your turn to help me out. *(Pause)* What did you tell her?

PESACH: I told her she was an angel sent by God. *(Quiet chortle)* I did!

(Blackout)

Scene Two

(PESACH's *sickroom.* SARA *carrying bowl of soup, quietly singing "Shoo, fly! Don't bother me". She moves toward blanket-covered figure puts soup down. Taps on blanket; no response. She continues humming-singing. taps again. figure doesn't stir. Finally she whispers.)*

SARA: Pesach Rubenstein.

(PESACH *stirs.)*

SARA: Are you awake?

(PESACH *stirs again.)*

SARA: I have some soup for you.

(PESACH *opening his eyes.)*

SARA: Your Aunt Leah says I can't stay too long...

(PESACH *rubs his eyes, peers again, more awake now)*

SARA: I have soup for you. Potato soup.

(PESACH *looks around, as if asking who is she?)*

SARA: You need nourishment.

(PESACH *peers at the soup.)*

SARA: The soup is there. Take it.

(PESACH *looks at* SARA.)

SARA: You look better than before.

PESACH: *(Groggily)* Who are—?

SARA: I've been told I can't stay too long.

PESACH: You've been told properly.

SARA: Because you're a married man?

PESACH: *(Pause, still groggy)* How do you know I'm married?

SARA: *(She points to watch on floor near bed)* You have a gold watch. The traditional father-in-law gift. *(She picks it up)* Have your soup.

PESACH: *(Gazing at soup)* How can I?

SARA: You want me to leave first?

PESACH: I need a spoon.

SARA: Oh! *(Laughs, takes spoon from her apron)* I'm sorry.

(SARA waits, PESACH tries soup)

PESACH: This is good.

SARA: Your Aunt Leah made it. Not me.

PESACH: *(Eating)* You can't make soup?

SARA: I'm a terrible cook.

PESACH: Then how will you find a husband?

SARA: *(Laughs)* Not through my cooking! *(Beat)* I'd better go.

PESACH: If you're helping a sick person, it's permitted to be here.

SARA: *(Suspicious)* You're sure?

PESACH: I'm a scholar.

SARA: No, you're not. You don't have pale white skin.

PESACH: I used to have pale white skin—when I was studying to be a rabbi.

SARA: *(Sneer)* A rabbi. I don't have a high opinion of them.

PESACH: Who do you think you are!

SARA: Sara Alexander.

PESACH: Listen, Sara Alexander— *(Coughs)*

SARA: *(She looks concerned.)* I'm sorry. You shouldn't... talk.

PESACH: *(Recovering)* I'm all right.

SARA: We thought, I mean, they—your aunt and your cousin—they thought awful things, you know.

PESACH: What awful things?

SARA: You might die.

PESACH: I disappointed you.

SARA: *(Laughs)* No! I'm glad you're better.

PESACH: Why?

SARA: Otherwise, I wouldn't be considered a very good nurse.

(PESACH *chuckles, coughs,* SARA *looks worried.*)

PESACH: A good nurse wouldn't make me laugh till I cough. *(He goes back to soup, sneaks looks at her.)* When I woke up, I..I didn't know who you were.

SARA: Who did you think I was?

PESACH: An angel God had sent.

(SARA *looks pleased.*)

PESACH: But God would never send a non-believer as an angel.

SARA: Now I have to go. You're fine.

PESACH: But wait...

SARA: Your Aunt Leah will be furious. She said to spend no more time than was absolutely necessary.

PESACH: But..But ..you can't go yet. *(Suddenly holds up bowl)* This soup is...not *hot enough!*

SARA: *(Looks)* It was steaming hot a minute ago!

PESACH: Well, it's almost cold!

SARA: It's fine. Now finish it.

PESACH: *(As he spoons soup)* Does your father permit you to be so impudent?

SARA: My father? That's none of your business.

PESACH: You came over with him, didn't you?

(SARA *turns away*)

PESACH: Who then?

SARA: The Young Jewish Socialist Farmers of Warsaw.

PESACH: Who?

SARA: That's what we called ourselves. We decided to come here to be farmers because the Czar said Jews could not be farmers!

PESACH: (*Laughs*) Are you from Warsaw?

SARA: Where you're from's not that important any more.

PESACH: I'd like to know!

SARA: From near Lublin.

PESACH: A Chasidic girl? Why aren't you married?

SARA: I'm only nineteen!

PESACH: Nineteen? In Lublin, that's an old maid.

SARA: That's why I came here.

PESACH: You came here to be an old maid?

SARA: If I want to. You can be anything you want here.

PESACH: (*Grins*) I came because my uncle wrote there was gold in the streets.

SARA: Poverty in the streets is more like it. (*Curious*) That's not really why you came? (*Beat*) I'd be disappointed if you said yes.

PESACH: I certainly didn't come here to abandon the Laws of Moses— (*Sarcastically*) —the way some people do. (*Beat*) You're not even kosher, are you?

SARA: I take meals at my new job—in a gentile house. Delicious food you don't even know exists.

PESACH: They hired a Jewish girl?

SARA: *(Chuckles)* They think I'm Polish. *(She heads off.)*

PESACH: *(Calls out)* How can we find a good husband for you if you're so disrespectful?

SARA: *(Turns, surprised)* Find a husband!!?? That's very funny!

PESACH: It's what you need.

(Skeptical look from SARA)

PESACH: An observant Jewish man you can depend on.

SARA: *(Snicker)* Depend?!! *(Continues exiting, humming "Shoo fly")*

PESACH: *(Calls out)* Wait!

(SARA pops back in.)

PESACH: What kind of song is that?

SARA: *(Turns)* Everybody's singing it. *(Sings)* "Shoo fly, don't bother me". Am I forbidden to sing a song, too?

PESACH: Is that a song for a Jewish girl to sing?

SARA: It's catchy, don't you think?

PESACH: I like Sabbath prayer singing. Melodies that go straight into God's ears. *(Sings)* "Shabbos..shabbos..." *(Coughs)* You should go to the synagogue.

SARA: I work on the Sabbath. *(Proudly)* In a brand new brownstone mansion close to Fifth Avenue. I'm the laundress. And third assistant cook.

PESACH: Where you eat pork?

SARA: And oysters!

PESACH: See! I'm right! You've turned against your own tradition.

SARA: *(Chuckles)* Tradition—you mean like agreeing the soup is cold because you're a man? *(Turns again)* Now I definitely must go!

PESACH: My Aunt Leah will be the matchmaker. I'll talk to her.

SARA: *(Laughing)* No, thank you!

PESACH: A strong and God-fearing man, that really is what you need!

(SARA struts out, blackout.)

Scene Three

(LEAH's parlor/workroom. Milliner's head form, hats, flowers, feathers, felt scraps. Knock at the door. She greets PESACH)

LEAH: Pesach! *(She hugs and kisses him)* Back on your feet *already*?

PESACH: I'm much better. No cough.

LEAH: From now on, you have to take care of yourself. *(Beat)* I'll get you some tea and some of my noodle pudding. *(She moves toward samovar)*

PESACH: *(Calling)* Your famous noodle pudding! It's why I came!

LEAH: If you came around more often, like you used to, I would cook for you.

PESACH: Well, I... It's just that...

(Uncomfortable pause, LEAH returns with tea and pudding, PESACH looks around.)

PESACH: Uncle Laibl is still away?

LEAH: I don't mind all that traveling he does.

PESACH: Dry goods is turning out to be a good business.

LEAH: It's as good now as he pretended it was in his letters to you. At that time he was picking rags up in the street. If not for these, *(Points to hats)* we would have starved.

(PESACH finishing pudding, uncomfortable silence)

LEAH: That's why you came? Just for noodle pudding?

PESACH: —and to thank you.

LEAH: Thank me? For what?

PESACH: For taking care of me when I was sick.

LEAH: You've already done that.

PESACH: Well, you deserve to be thanked again. *(Looking around)* I know what a problem I must have been. *(Points to hat forms).* You were so busy. And it's not as if I lived downstairs.

LEAH: If we don't have family to help, what do we have?

PESACH: But we also have *other* good people to help—

(LEAH pours tea, looks puzzled.)

PESACH: —like that girl you hired to look in on me.

LEAH: *(Spooning out)* Wait for your jam.

PESACH: That girl, remember? She brought me the soup. The girl with bad manners.

LEAH: You mean Sara?

PESACH: Sara, that was her name! A sad example of what can happen to Jewish people here.

LEAH: I'm glad you feel that way, too.

PESACH: Oh. Really?

LEAH: She seemed so bright at first. But—she turned out to be a disappointment.

PESACH: Why...are you disappointed?

LEAH: Such crazy ideas.

(PESACH *shrugs "so what?"*)

LEAH: And I hear she didn't keep the door to your room open the way she was supposed to.

(PESACH *another shrug*)

LEAH: Another thing, I heard she stayed too long in your room.

PESACH: Well...that's my fault! I...I...made her reheat the soup.

LEAH: I'll bet she boasted about eating pork at that fancy brownstone where she's working now.

PESACH: Clearly that girl needs to be helped!

LEAH: Helped?

PESACH: I mean disciplined.

LEAH: She's beyond help and certainly beyond discipline.

PESACH: Nobody is beyond help.

LEAH: A tramp? With a head full of socialist nonsense?

PESACH: That's exactly why we need to help her!

(LEAH *looks puzzled.*)

PESACH: I mean guide her...religiously.

(LEAH *still puzzled*)

PESACH: Otherwise she'll meet some gentile—and

LEAH: She's already become one of them.

PESACH: No, she hasn't. Not yet, but—

LEAH: Those kind, they step off the boat and throw off who they are—like it's an old coat full of lice.

PESACH: There's still hope with this Sara, I could sense it. If only someone would take her in hand.

LEAH: Who? Who could take her in hand?

PESACH: You!

LEAH: Me??!!

PESACH: *You.*

LEAH: There's nothing I can do for that girl.

PESACH: But there is...you could...teach her...teach her how to make noodle pudding like this.

LEAH: To make her more Jewish??

PESACH: Show her how to be a good Jewish wife.

LEAH: How about baked herring with potatoes, too? Maybe prunes with carrots? Pesach, we don't have time to be responsible for everybody, much as we're commanded to.

PESACH: There's a way we can help her, help everybody.

LEAH: What way?

PESACH: Make a match for her with an observant Jewish boy—

LEAH: *Make a match?* With *her*?

PESACH: Is there a better way to make her a good Jewish wife than to find her a good Jewish husband?

LEAH: First of all, I'm not a matchmaker!!

PESACH: In this country we all have to be matchmakers. There are so few real Jews here. Just Germans, Spanish.

LEAH: Second of all, she has no dowry!

PESACH: She has what any boy, and his family, should want in this country. She's a good girl, a smart girl who can learn what she has to.

LEAH: What nonsense!

PESACH: It's not nonsense. It goes for a blessing from God to do that .

LEAH: And who is the right boy? Who?

PESACH: Moshe!

LEAH: *(Shocked)* Moshe?

PESACH: Yes, Moshe.

LEAH: My Moshe, my husband's cousin's nephew?

PESACH: Shy, studious Moshe. Isn't he perfect?

LEAH: *(Dubious)* He's a scholar! One of the few we have here.

PESACH: How old is he?

LEAH: Twenty-one.

PESACH: Same age as me and I've been married for nearly two years.

LEAH: *(Skeptical)* And who's going to negotiate for her?

PESACH: I have an answer to that.

LEAH: Yes, who?

PESACH: Moshe's mother!

LEAH: *(Laugh)* How can his mother negotiate for both sides at once?

PESACH: She'll find a way.

LEAH: *(Nods knowingly, sadly)* Because the woman's so afraid she'll never have grandchildren, she'll do anything!

PESACH: But think of what would be accomplished— with a good husband this Sara would light candles, keep kosher, would cook on Friday so her husband can eat well on Saturday. She would listen and obey. She would do all the right things for the right boy. I'm sure of it.

LEAH: How do you even know she's willing, a girl like that?

PESACH: She is. I sense it. *(He reaches into his bag, pulls out prayer book)* I want you to give her this.

LEAH: That book was your mothers!

PESACH: Don't you think my mother would approve giving it to her as a start? Of course she would! She would have taken a poor stray like that girl Sara to her heart.

(LEAH looks askance, as PESACH holds out the book.)

PESACH: You must know where Sara works so you can give it to h—

(LEAH shrugs, she doesn't know.)

PESACH: Then you can find out from where she used to work!

(LEAH gestures "no way".)

PESACH: Give her the book.

(LEAH negative shrug again)

PESACH: If you're too busy, I'll try to find her.

LEAH: *(Suddenly shoves the book back into his bag)* Save your mother's book for your wife when she gets here.

PESACH: Rezl has her own book.

LEAH: Then with God's blessing and when the Almighty brings your wife here soon—you'll give the book to your first-born daughter.

(LEAH comes over, kisses PESACH, he's dejected)

LEAH: Pesach, stop worrying about strays. You're no longer tending your father's goats. *(She kisses again)* I'll get you more pudding.

(Crestfallen, PESACH rises to go.)

LEAH: Think of your own family, the people who love you. You don't even come over here any more!

PESACH: *(Laughs)* If you gave me those wonderful poppyseed cookies, like in the old country..

LEAH: I can make them for you again! Gladly! *(Pause)* Name the day. *(Pause)* Sunday. I can make them after Sabbath. *(Following him out)* You'll be here, then?

(PESACH shrugs assent.)

LEAH: Just like the old days—poppyseed cookies and Pesach.

PESACH: *(Laughs)* I'm glad I came to America—the only place to get your poppyseed cookies!

LEAH: You were in such a hurry to get here for the cookies, you had to leave the yeshiva?

PESACH: *(Kisses her)* If I *was* a rabbi, would the cookies taste any better? No!

(Blackout)

Scene Four

(Basement laundry room. SARA enters carrying wicker laundry basket, puts it down, returns to doorway, whispers out)

SARA: This way! Quiet!

PESACH: *(Slowly, cautiously enters, looks around)* Is it all right to be here?

SARA: They don't pay attention to the servant's entrance. Don't worry. *(Sorting laundered linens)* Sit!

PESACH: *(Curiously examining the room)* This is a gentile house? *(He continues to peer around.)*

SARA: Of course it is.

PESACH: You sleep here, too?

SARA: I have a tiny bedroom. *(Points next door, proudly)* But it's my own room. My first ever! *(Holds up her hands)* Before I slept in the ribbon factory basement. See! No rat bites here!

(PESACH examines SARA's hands.)

SARA: How are you doing?

PESACH: Good! Recovered. Thanks to you.

SARA: I believe we have a duty to take care of one another...

PESACH: *(Dismay)* You mean you would...take care of... just anybody?

SARA: I might. Depends.

(PESACH momentarily sad, recovers, pulls book out of his bag, SARA's curious, then astounded.)

SARA: A prayer book!?

PESACH: It belonged to my mother.

SARA: That's very sweet of you. But *(Puzzled)* that's why you were walking up and down the street, looking into every window? To give me a prayer book?

PESACH: Correct. To save you from outlandish ideas!

SARA: *(Points to book)* And that's how you're going to save me?

PESACH: My mother, a woman everybody respected, took it to the synagogue every Sabbath; you do the same thing!

SARA: You must be under some illusion...

PESACH: The illusion is yours—thinking you can run away from who you are.

SARA: If you want to change, you change. That's America. *(Points to book again)* That's really why you're here?

PESACH: Yes. To see that you walk once again in the shadow of God.

SARA: In my experience, Jewish women walk in the shadow of their husbands.

PESACH: That's exactly the point. A husband for you. That's why I'm here.

SARA: You're here to offer me a husband in addition to a book?

PESACH: Yes. Marriage is the sacred way to lead—

SARA: Marriage? It's a financial transaction between fathers.

PESACH: That's the least important part—

SARA: Besides—not everybody wants to get married!

PESACH: Of course they do. Take Moshe. He's the boy I have in mind for you.

SARA: Who?

PESACH: Moshe. An observant Jewish boy I know who never meets anybody.

SARA: Why not?

PESACH: He's...well he's shy.

SARA: *(Laughs)* That's it? You want to marry me off to some sad refugee in the study house who has no knowledge of the real world, who studies so much he'll have no time for his wife and family, who's not only painfully shy but ugly and shorter than me. *(Holds up sheet)* And has pale skin the color of this!

PESACH: He's not that short.

SARA: Besides, runaway girls like me don't marry observant boys like him or you for that matter, even if we wanted to. Not that I could think of a single reason why a girl would want to marry you!

(Footsteps, muffled voice)

SARA: Oh my God, somebody is coming down!

PESACH: I'll explain to them. *(Holds out prayer book as if it's an explanation)*

SARA: *(Whispers)* No! They'll take one look at you and run out for a policeman. Here! Quiet!

(SARA pushes PESACH under a table, covers it with bed linens. Whispers)

SARA: Quiet.

(PESACH's hand comes out holding book)

PESACH: Here.

SARA: *(She looks, whispers.)* We Polish Jewish girls don't learn Hebrew. It's too hard for us to learn.

PESACH: *(Whispers)* This is a translation; you can understand it.

SARA: *(Whispers)* We're scorned by men for wanting to learn and scorned again for not knowing. No, thank you!

PESACH: *(Whispers)* I marked this week's prayer portion for you. I want you to be thoroughly familiar with it when you sit next to Moshe's mother. In the synagogue.

SARA: *(Astounded, still whispering)* Moshe's mother??

PESACH: *(Whispers)* Yes, his mother will be there. With the women.

SARA: *(Whispers)* You are really serious!

PESACH: *(Whispers)* Of course!

SARA: *(Whispers)* Ridiculous. I'm not the kind of Jewish girl she wants for her son.

PESACH: All that doesn't matter. When she sees a pretty young girl with a prayer book next to her, know what she'll believe? That God put you in that seat! That He is making the match!

SARA: *(Whispers)* Are you crazy?

PESACH: *(Whispers)* God put you there to give her grandchildren! Beautiful grandchildren! That's what she'll believe.

SARA: You are crazy! *(She listens for sounds)* You can come out!

(PESACH comes out, normal voices.)

PESACH: Maybe Moshe's mind is dizzy with study, but his eyes work. When he meets you, he'll think you came from God, also.

SARA: I'm not going to the synagogue. Or having anybody's grandchildren. So take that book away.

PESACH: But you have no real beliefs yet.

SARA: I have beliefs!

(PESACH scoffs.)

SARA: I believe in ethical behavior, in shared wealth, in reason and science. In doing good.

PESACH: How about beliefs in the Laws of your people!

SARA: My people are American! *(She points to book.)* Besides I burn prayer books!

PESACH: Is that your idea of a joke?

SARA: No! I burned my mother's book when I was fourteen.

PESACH: That's a sin.

SARA: God ignored her prayers to bring my father back—If there is a God.

PESACH: IF there is a God!??? IF there is a God! *(Angered, he puts on prayer shawl.)* There is! I know there is! Every morning, I talk to Him when I put this on! No matter how cold it is, it's warm under this shawl. On the holy days, when the ram's horn calls us to prayer there's no sweeter music in the world. *(Binds forearm with thin black prayer strap)* And I love binding my arm with the word of God. Because He told me to do it. That's the kind of life I want for you, which Moshe will want to share with you.

SARA: Not everybody wants that life! I myself saw pious Jewish women tossing their wigs into the water when the boat came into New York harbor.

(PESACH sighs sadly.)

SARA: Pesach, I'm sorry you're disappointed, particularly because you seem to have spent so much time looking for me.

PESACH: I would have spent *more* time, if I had to. This is important. *(Holds up book)*

SARA: Why didn't you just ask Leah where to find me?

PESACH: She didn't know.

SARA: Of course she did. I gave her the exact address when I quit my job delivering the ribbons.

PESACH: *(Puzzled)* Are you sure? *(He moves toward door, turns, waits, holds out book.)*

SARA: If you want to see me again, please could we do it without prayer books?

PESACH: But...what other reason would I have to see you?

(PESACH exits reluctantly. SARA turns back to her work, then, changing her mind, runs out, calling him.)

SARA: *(Offstage)* Pesach Rubenstein! Wait! Wait! I have ...questions for you.

(SARA *returns,* PESACH *in tow)*

SARA: The synagogue...your synagogue...they have women there?

PESACH: We're not Chasids. You're welcome.

SARA: They're upstairs? Behind a curtain?

PESACH: Yes, but God is upstairs, too. Moshe's mother, once she spots you—a pretty Jewish girl alone—she won't let you leave her side. She'll love you.

SARA: I'm just afraid I'll end up acting like a fool. Saying something stupid, or worse...insulting. Our women never went to synagogue.

PESACH: If you're smart enough to fit in with all those crazy socialists and Jewish Enlightenment geniuses you won't have any trouble with nice Jewish ladies who fuss over a pretty girl. Besides, I can teach you all you need to know in a short time.

SARA: You're going to teach me? Us together, alone? It's not permitted.

PESACH: That's correct! *(Beat, recovering)* That's why I have a plan.

SARA: *(Skeptical)* What plan?

PESACH: A public place. Leah can't say we were alone then.

SARA: Where?

PESACH: Right down the street here.

SARA: The little park? Yes. That's a nice spot...

(PESACH *turns to leave again,* SARA *holds out her hand, gesture of goodbye and equality, he looks at her extended hand, holds it.)*

PESACH: The sages say—to look at the finger of a woman is to look at her whole body naked.

(PESACH *pulls hand back, bolts, blackout.*)

Scene Five

(LEAH's *parlor/workroom. She's trimming a hat. There's a knock, she crosses,* SARA *at door*)

LEAH: Sara.

(SARA *enters.*)

SARA: You wanted to see me.

LEAH: Yes. Sit down. *(Sits)* The girl who replaced you at the ribbon factory—they say she's lazy—

SARA: I don't underst—

LEAH: If you want I could—

SARA: Oh, I see. Thank you. But, I like my new job. I thought you knew.

LEAH: I...I wasn't sure.

(SARA *puzzled, turns as if to leave.*)

LEAH: Let me get you some tea. *(She exits.)*

SARA: *(Examining hats; to offstage)* Mrs Sklarky, at the ribbon factory, they always said you do the best work! *(She holds up a hat)* Beautiful!

LEAH: *(Offstage)* Without children, I have plenty of time—

SARA: Three, I heard.

LEAH: *(Offstage* Pesach told you that?

SARA: They all died, he said.

LEAH: *(Offstage)* Two before birth. The third, born dead.

SARA: I'm so sorry.

LEAH: *(Returning with tea)* A little boy, with beautiful blond hair.

SARA: It's probably good you came over—to a new place.

LEAH: It wasn't an easy decision. The rabbis back home who call America the impure land, they knew something.

SARA: *(Drinking)* Pesach says he loves your noodle pudding.

LEAH: I have some, would you like it?

SARA: No thank you. *(Pause)* He told me he likes your poppyseed cookies, too.

LEAH: Really? He tells you about those, also? *(Another nervous pause)* I wanted to ask you—these religious lessons—Pesach, I'm sure, is a good teacher.

SARA: Excellent. He could have been a rabbi I think.

LEAH: We expected that would happen. *(Pause)* As a rabbi, he would tell you you don't need so much knowledge of the Law to be a good Jewish woman.

SARA: But you're very smart in the Law. *(Beat)* I hear you bribed your brothers to teach you what they learned.

(LEAH cautiously acknowledges)

SARA: I admire resourceful women.

LEAH: *(Surprised)* He told you all that, too? What else does he say?

SARA: Nothing really. Only he's grateful you helped bring him here.

LEAH: *(Embarrassed laugh)* My husband Laibl filled his head with nonsense about getting rich in America! Even while he was in the yeshiva!

SARA: But if you preferred Pesach to stay there and finish up, why didn't you stop your husband? *(Uncomfortable silence)* Well, he is pretty.

(LEAH taken aback)

SARA: I mean—well, handsome. *(Long pause, gets up to go)* I mean is there anything more I can—

LEAH: *(Arises)* You might ask him when you see him why I haven't seen him in a month.

SARA: Maybe...he's..busy...with his new business.

LEAH: New business?

SARA: Oh. *(Nervous)* Don't you know? *(Hesitates)* He gave up peddling threads and notions and those cheap scarves.

LEAH: Really? So what's he doing?

SARA: Selling goat cheese.

LEAH: What?

SARA: To restaurants and at markets.

LEAH: *(Puzzled)* Whose cheese?

SARA: A Polish goat farmer in Brooklyn. Pesach found a stray and returned it and the two started talking. Pesach said the man's cheese was wonderful...

LEAH: Not better than his father's.

SARA: Better than anything in America. That's what Pesach says. In fact, that's how his new business started.

LEAH: *(Frosty)* Really? He used to tell me those things.

SARA: I wish he had.

(SARA moves to go, LEAH stops her.)

LEAH: Before you go—I just got a new picture of Rezl from her family, and a letter from Pesach's father.

(SARA *gestures no, but* LEAH *exits anyway.*)

LEAH: I'll show you the picture I got.

SARA: I really have to go.

(LEAH *returns waving picture, holding out letter.*)

LEAH: His father writes the greatest joy any father can have is knowing his children are leading a pious life!

SARA: I should go.

LEAH: He's almost totally deaf, you know. Poor man. The golden chain of Rubenstein rabbis—two hundred years—broken! Twice! Once the father. And then again—Pesach. (*Holds picture up to* SARA*'s face*) Look, Pesach's wife, Rezl! I hear she desires children. That's good news, don't you think?

SARA: (*Puzzled at first*) You think that will give her the courage to come here?

(*As* SARA *exits*)

LEAH: (*Brusquely*) She'll be here, very soon. I can assure you of that!

(*Blackout*)

Scene Six

(SARA, *sitting at river's edge. Picnic basket. Foghorn sounds.* PESACH *enters.*)

PESACH: The ferry man says in an hour.

SARA: (*Nervous laugh*) I thought you left me and went back to Manhattan.

PESACH: (*Laughs, sits*) And give up the pleasure of teaching you to believe what you refuse to believe?

SARA: Abraham and Isaac on the mountain?

PESACH: The greatest single lesson of all!

SARA: A father willing to sacrifice his son?

PESACH: Exactly. Is there any higher expression of faith in the Lord!

SARA: *(She holds up book)* I like Job's story. Undeserved suffering! That's easy to believe.

*(*PESACH *laughs,* SARA*'s serious.)*

SARA: Pesach, I appreciate your teaching me. Leah's probably right about you being a great rabbi.

*(*PESACH *winces.)*

SARA: But, honestly, all your teaching goes in one ear and out the other.

PESACH: That's because your head's full of—what's his name, Marx. There's no room for Moses. We're changing that!

SARA: To me there is only one lesson: we are responsible for each other. *(She points.)* Take those bridge workers out there. Nineteen of them have lost their lives working on that bridge. They are our problem. Not what's in an old book. *(She waves.)* Hello, comrade!

PESACH: *(Upset)* A girl shouldn't do that!

SARA: *(Chuckling over his stuffiness)* Of course I should. *(She points.)* Those men—when you pray, do you pray for God to help workers?

PESACH: Of course I do. The deserving workers. Always.

SARA: Do you pray that God will help the rich?

PESACH: Yes. The deserving rich.

SARA: Then you definitely ought to hear Feingold's lecture—

PESACH: I suppose he says there are no deserving rich?

SARA: More or less.

PESACH: *(Chuckles)* You mean if I do well, I'm a devil!

SARA: That's a possibility.

(PESACH laughs.)

SARA: You definitely should come to another meeting—

PESACH: Once was enough for me. Those people won't even admit the possibility God exists.

SARA: *(Upset)* Those people are...my...are like my family!

PESACH: Those people destroy families. Because of them, I lost an older cousin I loved. Ezra. He stood up in the synagogue one day. God is not the creator of the Jewish people, he said, the Jewish people created God. My family said the prayer for the dead over him and not soon after he left our village.

SARA: *(Angry)* Your own flesh and blood?! You did that?? Chased him out?

PESACH: Socialism, anarchism, Enlightenment—they turn good people against each other. Even cousins who love each other.

(SARA nods no!)

PESACH: Yes!! They do!

SARA: You're wrong! Those are good people. *(Beat)* With a few exceptions.

PESACH: They're not your family. Your family is your family.

SARA: In your case!

PESACH: *(Puzzled)* What does that mean? You don't miss your mother, your father?

SARA: My father is...is, well, he's gone. Out of my life..

PESACH: He died?

SARA: No, he went away. Left me when I was seven!

PESACH: *(Shocked)* Never...came back?

SARA: No!!

PESACH: *(Head shakes sadly)* Growing up without a father—

SARA: Until I got a little older, a day never passed when I didn't go to the door in the morning, expecting to see him coming back.

PESACH: Your mother never had a word from him?

SARA: Some people swore they saw him in Warsaw, where he used to deliver cotton goods.

PESACH: *(Pause)* I hope you don't mind me asking—

SARA: I know what you're going to ask. Did he leave for another woman? *(She shrugs: "who knows?")* I used to think he left for another little girl. I hated her!

PESACH: And your mother?

SARA: He never sent her a divorce writ. The rabbi never knew where to find him—

PESACH: So she could never remarry?

(SARA nods yes.)

PESACH: Poor woman.

SARA: *(Smiles)* Poor is right. We were so poor we had to take in a boarder, a distant cousin.

PESACH: *(Curious)* Why are you smiling?

SARA: Soon, the boarder took to my mother's bed, like man and wife! He was where my father was supposed to be.

PESACH: *(Shocked)* This man—did he treat you all right?

SARA: He was crazy. A terrible gambler, so we were just as poor as we ever were. One day he decided I was the reason for his bad luck. He wanted me to hide when he was around.

PESACH: *(Shocked)* But your mother stood up for you!

SARA: *(Laughs)* No! She was scared he was going to leave her. So I decided it was time to go find my real father.

PESACH: You went to Warsaw?

SARA: I knocked on every door in the ghetto. But all I found: boys and girls on the corner making a racket. Socialists. Anarchists. Some begging money to go to Palestine. One, who used to be a rabbinical student, claiming we were not descended from Adam and Eve, but from monkeys!

PESACH: *(Amused)* Monkeys!

SARA: Don't laugh. For the first time I felt like I belonged somewhere.

PESACH: Are they the ones you came here with?

SARA: Yes. No. *(Pause)* I mean—part of the way. *(Pause)* It's complicated. On the ship— *(Hesitates)* you know how dangerous it is down below. This boy Isaac from our group said he'd look out for me. I should have known.

PESACH: *(Questioning)* Should have known...?

SARA: He tried to—you know what he tried to do, and then when I said *no!* He hit me.

PESACH: *(Shocked)* What!! I can't believe somebody you knew—

SARA: *(Slight chuckle)* Wait! He was so shocked when I punched him back, I was able to sneak away.

(PESACH shakes head in sadness.)

SARA: I'm lucky! People say many girls coming over alone just disappear.

(Pause, both speechless)

SARA: You can stop giving me lessons or seeing me at all now, if you want.

PESACH: *(Puzzled)* Why? Why should I do that?

SARA: Because you don't believe that I punched Isaac and ran away.

PESACH: *(Confused)* I don't??

SARA: People tell lies about socialists, that we're for what they call...you know, free love.

PESACH: *(Puzzled)* If you were afraid I wouldn't believe you, you wouldn't have told me the story in the first place!

SARA: I have to know you believe me!

PESACH: I do. I believe everything—but I can't believe you'd still be with those people.

SARA: I'm in a different group here. Wonderful people. Asa—the one you saw—he's our leader. A brilliant man.

PESACH: Asa. You call him by his first name—

SARA: We're all friends.

PESACH: You're friends?

SARA: Friends.

PESACH: I'm not jealous or anything.

SARA: I never said you were jealous. Moshe, my intended, should be jealous.

PESACH: Moshe? *(Nervous laugh)* What do you mean jealous? You two haven't even met yet. You just sat next to his mother one time in the synagogue. That's all.

SARA: When Moshe finds out how much time you spend with me, he'll be plenty jealous.

PESACH: How do you even know that?

SARA: I'll find out Friday night, won't I?

PESACH: Friday night? What's happening Friday night?

SARA: His mother's going to introduce me to Moshe after the service. Then—the following week if everything goes well, I'm invited over to bless the candles and have sabbath supper with them.

PESACH: You're going to meet Moshe?

SARA: That's the idea, isn't it?

PESACH: Much too early. You need to acquire more learning, more love for—

SARA: She doesn't feel that way.

PESACH: Did you tell her about Karl Marx?

SARA: Oh, Yes. She asked me about him.

PESACH: What did she ask?

SARA: If he was Jewish.

(PESACH's *scratching his head as* SARA *snuggles close.*)

SARA: Pesach, I want to thank you for finding me a prospective husband.

(PESACH *shrugs uncomfortably.*)

SARA: My mother used to tell me nobody would ever marry me because I had no dowry. So it's very important to me to know that somebody—

PESACH: You're not ready yet to be married to such a pious boy, you realize that!

SARA: *(She kisses him)* There, that's just to tell you how much I appreciate your help. Now I can fulfill God's command to be fruitful and multiply. Moshe and I will bring grandchildren into the world. Six. Maybe ten.

(PESACH *sags, depressed.*)

SARA: What's the matter? It's your scheme, and it's working.

PESACH: Why do you want to do this?

SARA: I thought you wanted me to do it.

PESACH: I do—I did—yes of course, I do and I'm a man of my word, but it's moving too fast.

SARA: Why are you so sad?

PESACH: I'm not sad. Do I look sad? I'm just...just hungry.

SARA: *(She opens basket)* I do love sitting here by the way! When Moshe and I are married, I'll bring our children here. By that time the bridge to Brooklyn will be finished, we won't even have to take a ferry! I can tell my children stories about how poor Irish men were slaves to the capitalist builders of the bridge and gave their lives.

(*As* PESACH *is stunned,* SARA'*s taking out food.*)

SARA: I have wonderful food today. You're lucky our cook's so generous. *(She reaches in and pulls out oysters.)*

PESACH: What is that!

SARA: Oysters. She gave me some. She said to eat them right away!

(PESACH *stares,* SARA *takes out lemon, squeezes.*)

SARA: See, you put lemon on them.

PESACH: This is how you practice to be a good Jewish wife to a scholar?

SARA: I have chicken, too.

PESACH: Kosher chicken?

SARA: No. But I brought you an apple, a pear, and—I'll bet you never had this before... *(Takes out banana)* a banana...

PESACH: I brought bread!

(SARA sucks an oyster, PESACH's still dumbfounded at the sight.)

PESACH: Tell me something— *(Points into basket)* Is that chicken there from a hen?

SARA: *(Puzzled)* Does it make a difference?

PESACH: As boys, we couldn't bring chicken into the study house for lunch unless it comes from a rooster.

SARA: You mean because a female is not allowed in the study house?

PESACH: That's right!

SARA: See what I mean! See how ridiculous—

(Sly smile comes over PESACH's face, SARA realizes he's joking, she throws an oyster shell at him.)

SARA: You tricked me!

PESACH: *(Laughs)* It's easy to trick people who think they have all the answers!

SARA: I have all the answers? Me??

(SARA throws more shells at PESACH, blackout.)

Scene Seven

(SARA in her room, hears knock, opens door. LEAH is there.)

SARA: *(Surprised)* Mrs Sklarsky! *(Puzzled)* Is it Pesach; is he all right?

LEAH: *(Enters)* I'm afraid you know more about that than I do.

SARA: *(Taking off her blouse)* I have to get dressed. I'm going out.

LEAH: You're using Pesach's "lessons" as an excuse to be with him, aren't you?

SARA: I'm learning to be a good religious wife.

LEAH: All the rumors say something else—your so-called lessons are anything but!

SARA: People have too much time on their hands. So they make up stories.

LEAH: I heard these from reliable, upstanding people!

SARA: There's nothing I've done or Pesach's done we're ashamed of!

LEAH: Has Pesach been conducting these lessons he gives you here? *(She points to bed.)*

SARA: Here in my room. In that bed? No! *(She continues dressing.)*

LEAH: He has never been here?

SARA: No! He's never been here. He never will be here. I think it's time you left.

LEAH: I have a duty.

SARA: You have an unnatural interest in a grown man, if you ask me!

(PESACH, at a distance strolling on, unseen at first)

LEAH: You keep a decent tongue!

SARA: And *you* think I'm acting scandalously? A woman your age.

LEAH: *(Shocked)* How dare you!

SARA: The possibility that I'm not telling the truth, that Pesach has been in that bed—that's eating your heart away, isn't it? I feel sorry for you.

(Furious, LEAH *slaps* SARA, *who's about to return blow, holds back.)*

SARA: Get out of here!!!

LEAH: Tell Pesach that I had to punish you. You tell him the minute he gets here!

SARA: He doesn't come here. I told you! He will never come here!

*(*PESACH *arrives starts to knock, hesitates as* SARA *opens the door to usher* LEAH *out.* LEAH *stunned)*

LEAH: Your father would be horrified!

SARA: I told you the truth! He's never been to my room before!

PESACH: *(Calling out to* LEAH*)* Leah!! *(He runs out after her)* Leah! Wait! You don't understand!

*(*SARA *slams door,* PESACH *returns, knocks.)*

SARA: *(Opening door)* Please go away. This is not the time.

*(*PESACH *steps in,* SARA *covers herself with a blanket.)*

PESACH: I've been thinking a lot about—

SARA: I'm not dressed!

PESACH: About Moshe's mother. About Moshe—

SARA: What about him?

PESACH: I don't think it's right.

SARA: *You* don't think. Well, it's none of your business now. And what are you doing here, making me into a liar?!

*(*SARA *starts to shove* PESACH.*)*

PESACH: *(Stunned)* I have things to say to you—

SARA: I told you I'm going out tonight. To Moshe's mother's. To meet my intended.

(PESACH *confused*)

SARA: They're very sincere people.

PESACH: But you can't. It's wrong.

SARA: Out!

(SARA *pushes* PESACH *hard, closes door on him. He opens it.*)

PESACH: Why should I leave?!

SARA: Because I don't want you here! Because you shouldn't be here! Moshe's mother is waiting for me. She's waiting word. She wants to know, what do I think of Moshe? (*She pushes him out. Slams door*)

PESACH: (*Calling, outside door*) You already met Moshe?

SARA: (*Cool*) Yes.

PESACH: (*Calling*) When?

SARA: His mother introduced me. Last week. Outside the synagogue. I told you it would happen. She hopes to discuss things tonight, after the dinner.

PESACH: (*Calling*) Did you tell her that people in your group were arrested?

SARA: Yes.

PESACH: (*Calling*) What did she say?

SARA: She told me where to buy the freshest whitefish.

PESACH: (*Calling*) That's all?

SARA: She told me challah was better when you make it without the egg whites.

PESACH: (*Exasperated, calling*) I'm going to tell her that this whole ridiculous idea was mine, not yours.

SARA: Why bother? She's very happy with me. With her future grandchildren.

PESACH: *(Calling)* You're not really going through with this?

SARA: We're talking tonight. How many times do I have to tell you?

PESACH: *(Calling)* What are you going to say to her?

SARA: Pesach, do you think it's proper that I tell you?

PESACH: *(Calling)* Yes!

SARA: It's disrespectful to Moshe and his mother to tell you!

PESACH: *(Calling)* Disrespectful?

SARA: I can't let you in on my feelings about another man!

PESACH: *(Pause, calling)* You two wouldn't get along.

SARA: That's for me and Moshe to say.

PESACH: *(Calling)* I'm not going to allow it to happen. *(He bangs hard on door.)*

SARA: *(She opens.)* Stay out! This is my room!

(PESACH steps in.)

SARA: Moshe's a nice boy. Modest and unassuming. That's very becoming in a man.

PESACH: You're not ready for a scholarly boy like that. You'll both be miserable.

SARA: The object is to have babies, isn't it?

PESACH: But—

SARA: Babies change your outlook—

PESACH: He's so short, isn't he?

SARA: What does that matter?

PESACH: And he's not good looking. Did you notice!

SARA: Since when is that important?

PESACH: Pale blond beard. Weak looking face.

SARA: I hardly noticed.

PESACH: Pale white hands.

SARA: Unimportant.

PESACH: You're not ready!! You don't even know the prayers for the blessing after the sabbath ..

SARA: Good Jewish women are not supposed to be too smart.

PESACH: You don't really like him, you know!

SARA: On the contrary, he seems nice.

PESACH: That's all? Nice? What's nice?

SARA: Nice. Reliable. Not complicated.

PESACH: That's it? That's all. That's not enough!

SARA: Studying holy books all the time, that's good.

(PESACH *surprised*)

SARA: I'll know where my future husband is. That's important to me

PESACH: *(He pushes his way in)* Tell me the truth! What are you going to say to Moshe's mother tonight?

(SARA *tries to step around* PESACH *to continue dressing.*)

SARA: I said I cannot talk to you about it!

PESACH: Then you're not going there!

SARA: You can't stop me from going. You have no right.

(PESACH *bars* SARA*'s way, she tries to step around him.*)

SARA: And don't think you're going to change my mind with something from the Bible or some rabbi from a thousand years ago. I'm on to that eternal wisdom business of yours!

PESACH: Maybe you do need to hear something from the Bible right now. A message with the power to bring you to your senses.

SARA: I've had enough of your exalted teachings.

PESACH: The first time I saw you I thought of the poetry of David in the wilderness of Judah—

SARA: And what did King David have to say—there goes Sara, the tramp.

PESACH: King David said, "My flesh longs for you".

(SARA *stops, transfixed.*)

PESACH: I say the same thing. *(Beat)* "My flesh longs for you, my soul thirsts for you like in a dry and thirsty land...

SARA: *(Stunned, slowly)* "...where no water is..

PESACH: You know it?

SARA: I used to see it my mother's book, before I burned it. I always wondered what they meant by "flesh." I used to squeeze my arm to see if flesh could get thirsty.

PESACH: *(Closer)* I think all the time about squeezing your arm.

(*Suddenly* PESACH *and* SARA *are very close. They embrace, kissing, hugging, clutching. Then she turns away.*)

SARA: No. You're not free for this..

(PESACH *pulls* SARA *to him, kisses her hard and long, she returns hug and kisses intensely. She whispers as they continue to kiss and hug.*)

SARA: My arm...that really came into your mind when you first saw me?

(PESACH *nods yes.*)

SARA: When you were peeking at me from under your blanket?

(PESACH *nods yes again,* SARA *laughs joyously, kisses him, breaks away.*)

SARA: You've been longing and thirsting a long time.

PESACH: Yes.

SARA: So have I.

(PESACH *and* SARA *resume caressing, start to undress each other, he stops at the inside fringed prayer vest he wears under his shirt, takes it off, puts it back on, finally taking it off and carefully placing it down. They drop to the bed, and continue to caress, she whispers.*)

SARA: Pesach, I feel guilty about Moshe's mother now. First thing tomorrow, I'm going to tell her how sorry I am. I'm going to say she should look for a proper Jewish girl for Moshe, one with ideas that don't frighten everybody.

(*More disrobing, fondling, kissing, snuggling, gradually fade as* PESACH *and* SARA *begin physical lovemaking*)

END OF ACT ONE

ACT TWO

Scene One

(1875, PESACH's *cell,* STEPHENSON *enters, rushes toward* PESACH. LEAH *with food basket follows.)*

STEPHENSON: Damn you! Damn you! Damn you!

LEAH: Mister Stephenson, please.

STEPHENSON: I'm a good lawyer, Rubenstein. Respected in the courts of seven states. Feared by prosecutors, hired by other lawyers to save their failing cases. What are you trying to do? Make a fool of me?

PESACH: No.

STEPHENSON: Do you know what just happened in court!! Do you care!!

LEAH: Mr. Stephenson, this coroner, how does he even know the baby was from Pesach?

STEPHENSON: He doesn't. To the jury what does that matter?

PESACH: It was my baby! It had to be!!

STEPHENSON: She never told you?

PESACH: No.

STEPHENSON: Are you sure?

PESACH: Yes, I'm sure.

LEAH: Maybe she didn't even know. The first weeks of life.

STEPHENSON: In the jury's eyes it's now an open and shut case! You killed her because your wife was on her way to America and Sara was carrying your baby.

LEAH: He killed her because she was pregnant when— who knew she was even pregnant??!

STEPHENSON: There is only one way to turn this trial in your favor, Rubenstein. Those jurors have to be near tears, out of love or understanding for *you* in my summation. It's why I'm here. Other lawyers hire me to make closing speeches in their trials. But before the jury knows Pesach, what's in his heart and head, I have to know! The milk of human kindness is the only weapon I have. The milk may be turning sour very quickly.

PESACH: What's in my heart? Nothing.

STEPHENSON: You don't think I'll understand because I'm a Christian? According to my bible, the Christian savior is a descendant of David. Your commandments are mine. Are we that far apart?

LEAH: Pesach, answer him!

STEPHENSON: Why did you run all the way back to the synagogue from Fulton Landing to tell them Sara was lying dead? You could have said nothing, packed your bags and skipped out to the west.

PESACH: Guard! Guard get this man out of here

STEPHENSON: I'm not going. And the guard isn't listening.

PESACH: Just go!!!

STEPHENSON: The only way you will get rid of me is for you to tell me what's in your heart and head at this very moment.

PESACH: Why? Why should I?

STEPHENSON: Because I haven't yet found a way to get the jury to give a damn about you.

(PESACH *turns away, to a corner of the cell, just staring into darkness.*)

STEPHENSON: I know what shame is. From my own life. I know what it is to hope never to look my people in the face again.

PESACH: I don't care to hear about that—

STEPHENSON: Well you're going to. My sister's son—

PESACH: Please, I'm not interested.

STEPHENSON: My nephew, seventeen years old, insisted on joining up. Against all military rules, I took him into my regiment—because my sister begged me to keep an eye on him! He was killed at Vicksburg, in a charge I ordered!

PESACH: You think you killed him? A war! Even in the Bible...

STEPHENSON: Unfortunately, I don't forgive myself that easily.

PESACH: *(Pause)* You mean *I* should?

STEPHENSON: Maybe we both should.

PESACH: Go! Leave! I don't want to talk about these things any more.

STEPHENSON: I told you the truth, whether you believe it or not. Now when you're ready to tell me your truth, let the jailer know.

(PESACH *looking away*)

STEPHENSON: Rubenstein, did you hear me?

(Offstage crowd noises)

STEPHENSON: Listen to them. They hang the condemned right outside.

(STEPHENSON *points toward gallows,* LEAH *moan-shriek*)

STEPHENSON: They put the gallows up and take them down when the show is over. Public entertainment. You'll be the show.

(LEAH: *moans again, as* STEPHENSON *approaches.*)

STEPHENSON: What do you think about that?

(*No answer still*)

STEPHENSON: What are you thinking about?

(*Silence still*)

STEPHENSON: Tell me!

PESACH: (*Musing*) That place.. the Garden of Eden.

LEAH: (*Puzzled*) The Garden of Eden?

STEPHENSON: You're referring to that meadow in New Lots where—?

PESACH: (*Smiles, distractedly*) Sometimes—there— she would look up and ask me if we could ever escape God's eyes.

STEPHENSON: You were there more than that one time?

PESACH: Yes.

STEPHENSON: Often?

PESACH: She loved it. She loved the way the willow tree branches dipped down into the brook. Like she imagined the Garden of Eden must have looked.

STEPHENSON: What did you do there?

PESACH: (*Wry sad laugh*) We played Adam and Eve!

STEPHENSON: You disobeyed the Lord—I mean at a time when you still believed in Him?

PESACH: Yes.

(PESACH *coughs, lies down on his bench, blackout.*)

Scene Two

(*Open field, trees.* SARA *on blanket, picnic basket nearby,* PESACH's *shirt and prayer vest are on ground. She's suddenly concerned*)

SARA: (*Calling*) Pesach! Where are you? (*She peers out*) Pesach!

(PESACH *finally appears, bare-chested, holding tin cup with water*)

SARA: (*Upset*) Where were you?

PESACH: I found a brook (*Points*) —about a quarter of a mile down there— (*Holds up cup*) —beautiful clear running water. Here try.

(SARA *turns away.*)

PESACH: What's the matter?

SARA: (*Still upset*) I don't know. I thought—

PESACH: Here, try the water!

SARA: Promise me you won't do that again.

PESACH: Do what?

SARA: Go so far away—without telling me.

PESACH: (*Kindly laugh*) It's your fault. I was looking for something kosher. (*Holds up cup*) Water!

SARA: (*Composed*) I might surprise you one day, and bring something you can eat beside fruit.

PESACH: I'm still waiting.

(SARA *takes* PESACH's *hand, they lie down gazing skyward.*)

SARA: Pesach did you and Rezl ever picnic in the woods, like this?

PESACH: Certainly not before we were married.

SARA: After?

PESACH: Certainly not after.

(PESACH *and* SARA *both laugh.*)

SARA: You never tell me anything about her and you.

(PESACH *shrugs, turns away.*)

SARA: Tell me!

(*No response*)

SARA: Start at the beginning—

(PESACH *still reluctant*)

SARA: Your engagement.

(PESACH *shrugs, again reluctant*)

SARA: Coming from a great rabbinical family—you must have been engaged early.

PESACH: Fourteen.

SARA: (*Surprised, then smiles*) What took you so long?

PESACH: They had to wait for my wife to be born.

(PESACH *and* SARA *both laugh.*)

SARA: Stop fooling.

PESACH: I'm not. Not about being fourteen anyway.

SARA: She was the perfect choice, Leah says. The rabbi's daughter from the next village. You the rabbi-to-be—

PESACH: (*Ironically*) Now, I'm selling cheese instead of presiding in my grandfather's rabbinical court. Did she mention that?

SARA: She never stops. But she still adores you.

(PESACH *shrug. He and* SARA *both laugh.*)

SARA: Does she adore your wife, too?

(Nervous chuckle)

SARA: Tell me about her.

(PESACH turns away, evasively.)

SARA: Your wife, I mean.

(PESACH shrugs, evasive.)

SARA: Tell me about how you two...

(PESACH again baffled)

SARA: ...you must have made love many times.

(PESACH embarrassed)

SARA: You were together almost six months.

(PESACH still uncomfortable)

SARA: How does it compare..to us?

(PESACH still silent)

SARA: How do I compare?

PESACH: *(He walks away.)* I don't remember.

SARA: Of course you remember. Come back!

(No response)

SARA: Your wedding night!! Tell me!

(PESACH turns, stares.)

SARA: I don't believe you don't remember your wedding night!

PESACH: Only dimly.

SARA: Tell me about it dimly. *(She gestures "sit down".)*

PESACH: What for?

SARA: I want to know. I love to hear about wedding nights.

PESACH: It...was...beautiful.

SARA: Really?

(PESACH *sits.*)

SARA: Are you telling me the truth?

(*Still no answer*)

SARA: You're joking. Tell me the truth.

PESACH: Nothing happened on our wedding night.

SARA: Something must have happened!

PESACH: Honestly. Nothing happened.

SARA: I don't believe you—

PESACH: I spent it outside our bedroom! In the hall, if you must know, the only way to stop the poor girl from sobbing.

(SARA *rapt*)

PESACH: The next morning she went back to her father's place while her aunts came looking for blood on our bed sheet, the way aunts always do. Poor girl, her father was furious at her. I felt so sorry for her.

SARA: So there was...no blood on the sheet the next morning?

PESACH: From my standing outside in the hall all night?

SARA: All those months you were together—was there ever—blood on the sheet?

PESACH: Nine weeks and four days later.

SARA: (*A touch of pride*) Two months and one day ago, there was blood on my sheet.

PESACH: I noticed.

SARA: See I told you the truth about that Isaac on the ship!

PESACH: You haven't told me the truth.

SARA: (*Upset*) What haven't I told you!??

PESACH: About the black eye you probably gave him!

SARA: *(Laughs, presently)* Pesach, your wife, did she love you?

(No answer)

SARA: Does she love you?

PESACH: *(Shrug "who knows?")* Everybody told her love would come in time. She believed that. So did I.

SARA: Did you love her?

(PESACH hesitates.)

SARA: A little?

(PESACH shrugs, "sort of".)

SARA: Do you love her?

PESACH: They're over there and I'm here so I don't have to think about that.

SARA: Pesach, do you love me?

PESACH: *(Beat)* Yes.

SARA: When did you find that out?

PESACH: The minute I saw you.

SARA: That was the same time you thought I should marry Moshe! *(Beat)* Pesach, you didn't fall in love with me out of gratitude, did you? I mean you were sick, then when you discovered you were still alive—

PESACH: For a smart girl, you ask too many silly questions.

SARA: I've got one more silly question.

(PESACH turns away.)

SARA: How can you love me and love your wife?

PESACH: I...didn't say I...I...loved her, did I?

SARA: You must have feelings for her.

PESACH: Of course I do.

SARA: Real feelings or just obligations?

PESACH: I don't know. The second, I guess.

SARA: To her family, too?

PESACH: To a long line of people.

SARA: Your father in law, the rabbi?

PESACH: Definitely!

SARA: And to the marriage contract no doubt.

PESACH: Yes. *(Pause)* So I have to tell them!

SARA: About us?

PESACH: My wife, her father, my father. I have to tell them all.

SARA: Don't they know enough already?

PESACH: I'll talk to a rabbi, too, as soon as I can find one.

(SARA's puzzled.)

PESACH: —the one from Fourteenth Street went back.

SARA: A rabbi? Does that mean you're thinking about divorce?

PESACH: Yes. Of course.

SARA: You plan to get married again?

PESACH: Yes!

SARA: To me?

PESACH: Yes!

SARA: You have to ask me first.

PESACH: Will you marry me? *(Beat)* When I'm free, I mean. Would you?

SARA: *(She hugs him, gleefully.)* Yes. Yes. Yes. Yes. and Yes! *(She covers him with kisses)* I can't believe I've fallen in love with a boy who prays all the time. *(Kiss more, she breaks away.)* Am I shameful?

(PESACH looks puzzled.)

SARA: I know women are not supposed to do what I do—show how much I want you.

PESACH: I know that. But it arouses me.

SARA: It doesn't take much to arouse you. My naked hand aroused you.

(SARA holds out her hand, PESACH kisses it, leading to another impassioned round as they roll over and he's on top of her. She looks up at him.)

SARA: Don't move. I love all your weight pressing down on me. Stay! Forever!

(SARA's legs wrap around PESACH. He kisses her more, she holds him tightly.)

SARA: Whenever I close my eyes and open them from now on—forever—I want you to be there! Will you be there?

(Fade to half light as PESACH and SARA freeze. Lights return, he is still sleeping, she is up.)

SARA: *(Softly)* Pesach, wake up!

(PESACH doesn't stir. SARA gambols around, as he starts to wake up she turns.)

SARA: Pesach, do you think Eden was this pretty?

PESACH: *(Awakening)* I was never there.

SARA: *(Laughs)* Pesach, am I Eve here, in this Paradise?

PESACH: Eve? The trouble maker? No, of course not.

SARA: Well I'm certainly not Adam! Then—who am I here?

(PESACH grins, SARA is puzzled, then:)

SARA: Oh you! I'm not the serpent. If anyone's the serpent, it's You!

(SARA *hugs* PESACH *as he arises, then she stops suddenly.*)

SARA: Pesach—can I ask you something you'd rather not talk about?

PESACH: After insulting me, no.

SARA: If you're here and your wife is there, then how do you get a divorce?

PESACH: What are you talking about?

SARA: How can you get a divorce if she's not here?

PESACH: What happens in Europe when a husband lives miles many away from his wife? One rabbi writes to another, and it's done.

SARA: From New York to Poland?

PESACH: It has to be possible. If you get all the terms, find a rabbi and negotiate though him, it's perfectly honorable.

SARA: The rabbi sends the writ of divorce, that's all?

PESACH: Yes! All according to the Law.

SARA: Just like that?

PESACH: Of course, I have to write to Poland ahead of time, explaining everything.

SARA: What if Leah is right and your wife is on her way—right now—and it's too late to write?

PESACH: (*Chuckle*) My wife is always on her way. We were on our way the first time when she changed her mind at the train station and ran back to her father. She's been on her way five times over the past eighteen months. But nothing ever happens. Read the letters I've saved. First, they located another family for my wife to travel with, then—suddenly—another letter— change of plans!

SARA: Don't send them a letter now. It makes me nervous.

PESACH: I have to write to explain how I'll pay back the dowry, don't I?

SARA: You'll have to sell a lot of cheese to do that!!

PESACH: *(Points)* The goat man of New Lots wants to buy my business for his married son—the one he's always complaining about. Maybe that would—

SARA: But those are your customers. You got them.

PESACH: We're going to need the money!

SARA: *(Sits up suddenly)* Pesach, I'm confused.

PESACH: You?

SARA: Am I engaged? Officially engaged, like other girls?

PESACH: *(Puzzled)* Yes!

SARA: *(Smiles)* I'm really engaged?

PESACH: Yes.

SARA: Even though I have no dowry. No father to strike a deal.

PESACH: Even though.

SARA: But you and I haven't exchanged gifts.

PESACH: *(Laughs)* We don't have to—

SARA: I have an engagement gift for you. I made it myself—in the kitchen.

PESACH: Ham salad, probably.

SARA: *(Opens basket)* No—It's kosher.

PESACH: Kosher? How—?

SARA: I made in it a brand new crock, all from dairy.

PESACH: *(He takes off cover)* Noodle pudding! *(Laughs, pleased, can't believe it)* Noodle pudding!

SARA: I was going to give it to you to take home. I hope you like it.

(PESACH *samples.*)

PESACH: It's good. Very good. My engagement gift will be— (*He unhooks gold watch from his jacket nearby.*) This is your gift.

SARA: (*Shocked*) Are you sure—?

PESACH: Take it. It's for you.

(PESACH *ties the pocket watch chain around* SARA's *neck.*)

SARA: It's all right to do this?

PESACH: In time, I'll return it to my father in law—

(SARA *frowns.*)

PESACH: But not before I replace it with a diamond ring!

(SARA *smiles,* PESACH *eats.*)

PESACH: But the watch or the ring—neither could ever be as valuable as your gift to me. (*Holds up pudding*)

SARA: That's such a nice thing to say. (*She springs up, does a little dance holding out the watch, as if showing it to trees. Suddenly is very serious.*) Pesach. Now that we're engaged, we have to talk seriously about your lungs.

(PESACH's *surprised.*)

SARA: You have to take care of yourself.

PESACH: I do take care of myself.

SARA: You don't! It's going to be my job to make sure you do!

PESACH: Feed me noodle pudding. It's very good for the lungs!

SARA: No! I'm serious. I worry about your health.

PESACH: Stop worrying.

SARA: Well, I do worry!

PESACH: Worry about the Almighty.

SARA: It might surprise you but— (*She looks heavenward.*)

PESACH: You? You're really worried about Him?

SARA: (*Points up*) I feel like a little girl sometimes— (*Points skyward*) —when I used to wonder if He could see everything we're doing down here. Can He?

PESACH: Of course He can!

SARA: Then He's looking down on us right now?

PESACH: Of course.

SARA: Listening to everything we say? (*Looks at her puzzled*) That is if you believe God is...is there.

PESACH: What are you trying to say?

(SARA *points heavenward.*)

SARA: Does He like what He saw today, what He heard?

(*No answer*)

SARA: Answer me!

(*Still no answer*)

SARA: Tell me what are you thinking?

PESACH: (*Laughs*) You won't believe what I'm thinking.

SARA: Tell me!

PESACH: I'm thinking about Moses in the desert.

SARA: (*Puzzled*) Moses? What does he have to do with—

PESACH: It was easier then to know to know whether you were doing the right thing or not.

(SARA's *puzzled.*)

PESACH: All you had to do was open your tent in the morning. If God didn't leave you any manna for breakfast, you had a warning.

SARA: I'll make you manna, every morning. Whatever it is!

PESACH: You must be manna because God gave you to me.

SARA: Pesach, do you really believe that our love must come from God?

PESACH: He makes all things happen, so that's what I believe!

(SARA *kisses* PESACH, *he suddenly pulls away.*)

SARA: Then it's all right—I mean we're all right.

PESACH: Yes, of course. (*He kisses her, then looks up at sun.*) We have to go!

SARA: But—why?

PESACH: (*Rises, tugs on her*) The evening service!

SARA: I'll only let you go if you promise to pray for your health.

(PESACH *looks at* SARA, *disbelieving.*)

SARA: I believe in prayer if it keeps you healthy.

PESACH: (*Laughs, but nervously*) God doesn't make transactions.

SARA: Then why do you pray?

PESACH: Why? Because I must. (*Again, he pulls her along.*) Come on! (*Looks skyward*) The sun is starting to go down. Time to thank God.

SARA: For what?

PESACH: For you.

(*Blackout*)

Scene Three

(LEAH's *parlor. She is blessing the sabbath candles, her head covered, hands over candles.* PESACH *outside approaches, stops, looks at letter in his hand, reads it again, folds it up, finally knocks.*)

LEAH: Pesach?!

(PESACH *kisses small prayer box on door post, enters.*)

LEAH: You still have time to kiss holy words. (*Sarcastic*) That's good.

(LEAH *returns to blessing,* PESACH *waits, then impatient, he waves letters.*)

PESACH: Do something about these!

(LEAH *gazes.*)

PESACH: Letters from home!

LEAH: Why should I? Considering what— (*Pulls his jacket open*) There! Can you tell me what time it is?

(PESACH *stunned*)

Where is your watch, Pesach? Your father-in-law watch? The gift of tradition.

PESACH: Obviously it's not on me.

LEAH: For two months, Sara has been seen proudly wearing it around her neck. Or is it just some watch that looks like the one your father in law gave you? (*Beat*) For a smart girl, she's not being very smart.

PESACH: Write! Tell them you were mistaken. All these stories are just...just gossip.

LEAH: But I'm not mistaken. Everybody knows -including you.

PESACH: Tell them it's...it's...silly talk.

LEAH: Silly talk? She seduced you! Who is she? Here by herself at seventeen; she stole a respected Jewish boy from a fine family!

PESACH: This is America. There are no more fine families.

LEAH: What do you think you're going to do, marry her?

PESACH: Legally, some day.

LEAH: *(Scornful)* Do you think any rabbi who finds out the truth would sanction such a marriage?

PESACH: Those things are for rabbinical courts to decide.

LEAH: A hundred rabbis would say *no*!

PESACH: And what would a hundred rabbis say about a wife who is unwilling to come over?

LEAH: She will come. She wants to come. Especially now that she knows. *(Finishing ceremony, setting table)* All around here are men—gentiles, too—waiting for wives to join them. They go to harlots. It may be shameful, but it keeps the family together until their wives and children arrive.

PESACH: I've been to harlots. They didn't make me laugh.

LEAH: A sanctified life is not about laughing. *(Holds him arms length)* Don't you have vows to your wife? To her father? Didn't you sign the marriage contract before God?

PESACH: *(He turns away)* I pray at the synagogue. I observe the Sabbath, but life doesn't stand still.

LEAH: But it must. The laws of Moses, the wisdom that great Rabbis breathed into those laws—that doesn't change. For you Elizabeth Street should be no different than—than—Ostrolenk, Luboml, or even Babylon.

PESACH: Even the angels of God when they came to Abraham, learned to eat the new food of the new land, Abraham's land.

LEAH: I think you ought to leave.

(PESACH *stunned*)

LEAH: I can't do anything for you.

PESACH: I won't leave. Tell them all these rumors are not—tell them anything. I need more time to—

LEAH: You want me to help you close your eyes and cover your ears!! Like a child who believes everybody has left the room when he does that!

PESACH: I need some time, that's all.

LEAH: I know...I know why you need time!

(PESACH *turns, surprised*)

LEAH: Laibl heard at the synagogue. You're trying to raise money! Why, Pesach? To flee? To abandon your wife forever?

PESACH: Just—write!

LEAH: I will not.

PESACH: Tell them I'm coughing again; you saw blood on my handkerchief.

LEAH: *(Shocked)* Pesach!

PESACH: *(Anguished)* No! It's not true.

LEAH: *(Alarmed)* Are you sure? You're not sick again?

(PESACH *nods no,* LEAH's *still worried.*)

LEAH: Promise me!

(PESACH *nods again.*)

LEAH: Pesach, I know what you've been going through.

PESACH: I can never repay you for helping to bring me here—But now things have changed. We're here, not there.

LEAH: *(Hugs him)* Pesach, who knows you better than me? Remember when you were little and everybody was frantically looking for lost Pesach. Who knew right away where to find you—hiding in the holy ark!

PESACH: But I changed—a lot. And things are... different here.

LEAH: Pesach, I'm begging you to reconsider. It's not because your father and grandfather had dreams for you! And it's not because I do too. I'm asking you for your sake; look at what you're doing.

(PESACH attempts to pull out of LEAH's hug, she holds on to him.)

LEAH: A year from now you'll bless me for what I just said.

(LEAH kisses PESACH, he attempts to pull away, again unsuccessfully.)

LEAH: I can't let you go! Pesach—

(PESACH finally pulls away, LEAH pursues him.)

LEAH: Think of your family. Your father—poor man. The grief you already caused him when you left the yeshiva.

PESACH: *(Sudden flareup)* I didn't cause him grief for doing that!!

LEAH: *(Aghast)* How can you even say that when everybody knows—

PESACH: I explained everything. I brought him the ear trumpet to make sure he understood. "Poppa", I said, "Like you, I'm not going to be a rabbi. I'm sorry if I disappoint you".

LEAH: *(Points to her ears)* Cursed by God first, now by his son.

PESACH: Wrong! He understood when I told him, "Poppa, if God saw fit to make you a goat keeper, then maybe God doesn't want any more Rubenstein rabbis."

LEAH: How dare you hurt him like that!

PESACH: I didn't hurt him. He expected to hear it. He was at peace with my decision.

LEAH: Nonsense! You want me to believe he'd endorse the end of what all of us were so proud of? What he was so proud of?

PESACH: "The two hundred year old reign of Rabbi Rubensteins in Ostrolenk"?

LEAH: Yes! He would never—!

PESACH: The people of Ostrolenk never forgave him his affliction; do you even know that?

LEAH: What are you talking about? The people of Ostrolenk—and the members of our family—held their heads high because for two hundred years our rabbis were famous far beyond the district. You know that!!

PESACH: I know *this*! How I know it—walking in the square on market day, holding my father's hand, the people of Ostrolenk would smile joyously at me—a little boy—certain of who I would be some day.

LEAH: What's wrong with that?

PESACH: Because instead of smiling at my father, too, they looked away from him! Not *at* him! They looked beyond him. As if it was his fault their only source of pride was gone. As if he wanted to be a goatherd instead of what the firstborn men in his family had been for generations: their rabbi! In the end, I didn't want to be what he couldn't be. I wanted to be what he was—just a religious man!

(PESACH *bolts, stops at prayer box on door, kisses it*)

LEAH: Where are you going?

PESACH: To my goat farmer in New Lots. I'm going to lower my price!

LEAH: Come back. You can't just close the door on...on everything! (*Goes to door, calls out*) You won't leave us. You're too afraid of being set adrift in this alien land. You're tied to the past the way we all are!

(LEAH *shaking her head sadly, blackout*)

Scene Four

(*Laundry room.* SARA *carries in a basket full of linens, begins ironing, singing "Shoo fly", presently* PESACH *bursts in.*)

PESACH: The money's coming. Another week—two at the most.

SARA: (*Startled*) All of it?

PESACH: Enough.

SARA: You mean we can—

PESACH: Move to Chicago!!

SARA: We're really going?

(PESACH *nods yes.*)

SARA: Can I believe you?

PESACH: (*Surprised, puzzled*) Of course you can believe me.

SARA: (*Gleeful, kisses him, turns, searches*) I just got a letter from there. A girl who used to work at the ribbon factory. She likes it there. And her husband can get you a job.

PESACH: That's the Jewish girl?

SARA: I told you about her. She's from my district in the old country.

PESACH: So the rabbi there is—?

SARA: One of our kind, I'm sure.

PESACH: We call on him the minute we get to Chicago.

SARA: The rabbi sends the divorce writ to Poland. And we start a new life! Isn't that what you said?

PESACH: Yes, I have a letter in my bag.

SARA: What letter?

PESACH: A letter I wrote to send to Poland.

SARA: A letter about what?

PESACH: About everything!

SARA: *(Worried)* You're telling them about me?

PESACH: Of course about you.

SARA: Leah's told them enough.

PESACH: They must hear it from me. The truth. Everything. How disappointed I've been that my wife refuses to join me. How things are different here in America. The dowry: my plan to pay it back.

SARA: I don't think you should send that letter!

PESACH: But I want to get everything out in the open. *(He takes letter out of his bag.)*

SARA: What for?

PESACH: For the sake of Jewish law. For the sake of my family's name, or what's left of it.

SARA: No! Send your letter after we're in Chicago. When the rabbi sends the divorce paper.

PESACH: And what if there is no rabbi there? *(Holds up letter)* They have to read what's in here now. Why it's happening. How I begged Rezl for months and months to come over.

SARA: Why are you telling them anything?

PESACH: Right after I met you, I wrote letter after letter to get her to come. Why? To stop me from doing what I wanted to do, love you.

SARA: Please, for this once, do it my way, and just let's leave. No letters, no law. *(She hugs him for comfort.)* We have a whole good life ahead of us if we just go about this quietly. *(Kisses him)* Please.

PESACH: *(Holds out letter)* All right! *(Tears it)* There! *(Scatters pieces)* We'll do it the way you want!

SARA: *(Hugs him)* Please don't feel bad about it.

PESACH: It's all right.

SARA: No, you're worried.

PESACH: I'm a free man. Torah law must have exceptions.

SARA: Do you really believe that?

(PESACH doesn't answer. SARA picks up letter pieces, trying to put them back together.)

SARA: Then Pesach—send the letter.

PESACH: No. I won't.

(SARA kisses PESACH, blackout)

Scene Five

(1875. Cell. STEPHENSON enters, holds paper.)

STEPHENSON: Do you read English?

PESACH: A little.

STEPHENSON: Then you know what this says?

(PESACH *nods yes.*)

STEPHENSON: It's a translation of the letter your father-in-law sent you, isn't it?

PESACH: I know.

STEPHENSON: The judge passed it to me. Do you know what that means?

(PESACH *shakes his head no.*)

STEPHENSON: It means the judge is trying to help us. He knows where this case is going. He wants you to plead for mercy right now.

(PESACH *looks away*)

STEPHENSON: Here read the letter. Read the part the jury's going to hear.

(PESACH *shakes his head no.*)

STEPHENSON: Read what your father-in-law wrote. He was in the courtroom yesterday, did you notice? *(Thrusts it at* PESACH*)* Go ahead, read it!

PESACH: I know every word of it!

STEPHENSON: *(Reads)* "...as a good Jewish husband, whose contract was signed before the rabbi and before God, Pesach, you must put that shameful girl out of your life forever."

(PESACH *turns away.*)

STEPHENSON: When the jury hears that, they're *not* going to ask themselves: wouldn't a man who murdered or intended to murder *burn* a letter like this? Not leave it around for evidence! They won't even remind themselves that without you, nobody would have found the body. Instead they're going to say to themselves: a married man, wife coming over, girlfriend pregnant—aha! He must have done what the coroner suggested he did. Put her out of his life forever! Do you know what else the jury's going to see—this afternoon, a model skeleton, a neck, the coroner will point to the little bone in the neck of that skeleton that, in the case of Sara Alexander, was so broken the girl couldn't breathe. Rubenstein, we have an offer that will keep you alive. In jail perhaps, but alive. It's my recommendation—my strong recommendation—that you take advantage of it. I don't want your blood on my hands!

PESACH: You want me to say to the judge I *murdered* Sara?

STEPHENSON: Just nod *yes* to the judge's question. Determine to live!!

(PESACH turns away again, after a long wait

STEPHENSON: Obviously I have no more business here.

(STEPHENSON *exits, end scene, fade)*

Scene Six

(Same "Eden" setting. SARA and PESACH lying in the same pose as before, gazing up at the sky.)

SARA: Pesach, did I ever tell you about my Aunt Malke?

PESACH: The one with red hair?

SARA: Beautiful, long hair. She was the only one who ever loved me—before.

PESACH: *(Kisses her hair)* You have nicer hair.

SARA: I'm serious! When she refused to cover her hair, she scandalized the whole village! I was so proud.

(PESACH continues kissing SARA's hair.)

SARA: Maybe I shouldn't have been so proud of being, you know, different.

PESACH: *(Raises himself, gazes at her)* You? The Socialist, anarchist, believer in monkeys?

SARA: I want to give all that up and believe whatever you believe.

(PESACH's startled, then pleased.)

SARA: I'm going to have an open mind in Chicago.

(PESACH nods, smiles.)

SARA: What's Chicago like?

(PESACH shrugs, SARA looks around.)

SARA: Will there be a fields and woods as nice as this?

PESACH: We'll find them.

SARA: *(Beat)* If we don't get work right away, do we have enough money?

PESACH: Barely. The railroad fare was more than I expected.

SARA: *(She gets up, looks around nervously)* The tickets! Where are they?

(PESACH points to his bag)

SARA: You're sure? *(She reaches over)* Can I see?

(PESACH shrugs yes)

SARA: I never saw what a railroad ticket looks like! *(She looks in, finds tickets but her attention is caught by something else in bag, an envelope. She pauses to examine it, then quickly holds up tickets, kisses them.)* Chicago! *(She peers back into bag.)* Pesach, you got another letter from Poland.

PESACH: *(Unconcerned)* I know.

SARA: *(She takes letter out)* You didn't even open it!

PESACH: What's the point?

SARA: *(She looks at him, puzzled, he gets up.)* I want to see what it says about me! "The Whore?" Last time your aunt called me Delilah!

PESACH: *(Tries to yank letter away)* Tear it up!

SARA: *(Evading him)* I want to see.

(PESACH tries to grab it again, again fails.)

SARA: I wonder what they say! *(She opens, quick look)*

PESACH: What's in it?

SARA: *(Quickly scanning)* Uh...nothing much.

(SARA Abruptly puts letter into her skirt pocket, turns away, PESACH's puzzled.)

PESACH: Should I read it?

SARA: Read it on the train, tomorrow. *(Quickly takes tin cup out of basket)* I'm thirsty! I'll go look for the brook myself!

(PESACH watches, curious)

SARA: You want some water, too?

PESACH: *(Points to her skirt pocket)* Perhaps I should look at it.

SARA: *(Moving, cup in hand)* When we're riding through Pennsylvania! You'll have plenty of time then.

PESACH: *(Follows her, reaches toward her skirt pocket)* Can I see it?

(SARA adroitly sidesteps, PESACH's puzzled.)

SARA: It's just another letter!

(PESACH gets closer. manages to retrieve the letter.)

SARA: That must be the hundredth letter you got since I know you.

PESACH: *(Scanning)* This is from her father, not from Rezl or my aunts.

SARA: You got a letter from him before.

PESACH: *(Scanning)* I think she's really coming this time.

SARA: *(Forced chuckle)* You mean like the other times?

PESACH: He's bringing her! That's a surprise, this news.

SARA: Everybody has news. I have news.

(PESACH's scanning, not listening)

SARA: I'm not sure, though. *(She touches her abdomen)* Too early to tell, few more days.

(PESACH continues scanning, still puzzled, SARA waits.)

PESACH: He sold his house. *(Looks up from letter)* A young rabbi is taking over in Luboml.

SARA: *(Pretending to pay no attention)* Did I tell you! Our friends in Chicago have located a place for us. Near them. A basement room. But it's cozy, she said. Isn't that something? Basement here, basement in Chicago! *(Strained chuckle)* I never get out of the basement!

(PESACH's still scanning.)

SARA: But we're not going to stay if there are rats, right? *(She starts to unpack.)*

PESACH: He hears my health is good, for which he thanks God. There are socialist outbreaks all over, strikes at the new factories. Lev Altchick's house in Ostrolenk was burned down. Things will not be good when the old Czar dies. The crown prince is no friend of our people. There are going to be pogroms again, he thinks. America is a better place for his daughter, he says.

SARA: *(Nervous chuckle)* Chicago is a better place for his son-in-law!

PESACH: They'll be here...in...less than a week!!

SARA: That's not possible. It's a long voyage, Pesach

(PESACH *examines envelope,* SARA *comes over.*)

PESACH: It was mailed from where the ship sails—
Bremerhaven—almost two weeks ago.

SARA: Think of that—they get to New York the same
time we get to Chicago! Isn't that a funny coincidence?
(Brave laugh) We'll be immigrants to a new home the
same way they are.

(PESACH *returns to reading.*)

SARA: Did I tell you, there's an indoor toilet! It's
upstairs, but we can use it on cold days. *(Beat)* Did you
hear me?

PESACH: *(Distracted)* That's good.

SARA: Please listen to me!

PESACH: I heard what you said, cold days.

SARA: Please! Stop reading and listen to me. *(She stops,
gets up, approaches him)*

PESACH: The toilet, you said—

SARA: *(Pushes letter aside)* Aren't you pleased about the
toilet?

PESACH: Yes, of course.

SARA: So why aren't you happy? I'm happy.

PESACH: *(He resumes scanning)* They'll be here. In this
country. In New York. In just a day or two. Maybe
three.

SARA: Stop reading that letter. And listen to me.

(SARA *tries to take letter from* PESACH, *he dodges.*)

SARA: Let me have it! *(She runs around him.)*

PESACH: No, you don't!

(SARA *succeeds in snatching it from* PESACH, *runs a short
distance.*)

Pesach: Sara, please give me that letter back. *(He approaches her)*

Sara: *(Holding back letter)* No. Because you're not paying attention to me!

Pesach: I need the letter, please!

Sara: Why?

Pesach: I need it.

Sara: What for?

Pesach: The name of the ship is there.

Sara: *(Stunned, unbelieving)* The name of the ship? What do you need that for?

Pesach: I have to go down to the ship agent's office.

Sara: Whatever for?

Pesach: To find out when the ship gets in.

Sara: *(Shocked)* What are you talking about?

Pesach: In order to be there at the pier when—

Sara: I know you're joking because the Chicago tickets are all paid for.

Pesach: They're good for fourteen days.

(Sara sighs, crestfallen.)

Pesach: Please let me have the letter.

Sara: No. *(Starts to tear letter)* No! We're leaving tomorrow, so you don't need this.

Pesach: *(Tries to stop her)* Stop! *(He scrambles for pieces.)* What's gotten into you?

(Sara pulls a ladle out of her handbag. Pesach stares unbelieving.)

Sara: Did you see this? I just got it this morning from the housekeeper. Our wedding gift. Now with my own soup ladle, I have to learn to make chicken soup when we get to Chicago. Or cabbage soup. Both! Why not both!

PESACH: Sara, listen to me, please.

SARA: You're not going to Chicago at all, are you?

PESACH: Of course I am. But first a Hebrew legal matter has to be taken care of. It's only right.

SARA: Right? Am I not right?

PESACH: You know very well, according to our laws she needs a writ of divorce from me. Otherwise she becomes what we call a "chained woman" with no chance to re-marry and start another life.

SARA: We're in America now. She can go to a judge.

PESACH: That's not our way, an American judge...

SARA: You worry about the legal rights of a wife who loves you so much she has to be dragged here by her father?

PESACH: She'll be here, soon. I have to deal with that...

SARA: The rabbi in Chicago—that was our plan.

PESACH: I told you—there may not be a rabbi there. Maybe for the German Jews—but not for us.

(SARA *starts to pack up, at first* PESACH *doesn't notice.*)

SARA: All our months together and I'm in a contest with your wife—a contest I will lose when the boat arrives.

PESACH: What contest? Stop talking nonsense. She was supposed to be too afraid to come, too afraid to leave her father's home. That's what her cousin wrote me. Who would have ever thought he'd bring her here himself?

(PESACH's *puzzled, watching, as* SARA *continues packing*)

SARA: So just like that you abandon all our plans, and probably abandon me.

PESACH: *(Surprised)* Abandon you? Of course not.

SARA: Like my father abandoned me to my crazy mother who then threw me out of the house. Why? Because the boarder she was sleeping with didn't want me around. That's the last time anybody does a thing like that to me. Including you.

PESACH: You think I'm like your mother? That's incredible.

SARA: Go down to the ship dock. Greet shy, obedient Rezl, only daughter of her loving father, esteemed rabbi. When he brings some ancient curse down on your head—you'll suddenly believe you *are* the criminal they accuse you of being. And you'll begin to believe I am the whore they say I am.

PESACH: We're going to be man and wife. In Chicago. I'll do it in the civil court if necessary, don't you understand?

(SARA closes basket with finality, PESACH points to it.)

PESACH: What are you doing?

(SARA removes watch.)

PESACH: The watch!

SARA: *(Flings it at him)* Here. You'd should be wearing this when you meet your father in law, the rabbi.

(PESACH Picks it up, tries to put watch back on, SARA rejects it. She starts to exit.)

SARA: *(Enraged)* You can rejoice now! They won't have to say the prayer for the dead over you now or cut your picture out of the family photograph, as if you never even existed. Like they did your socialist cousin Ezra!

PESACH: What are you doing? *(He blocks her.)* Where are you going?!!

SARA: *(She runs around him)* I'm going to see if I can get my job back, and my warm little room. If it's not too late.

PESACH: No! It's not safe in these woods by yourself. *(He blocks her.)* Please listen! I'm just trying to do the decent thing.

SARA: *(She stops in her tracks)* Decent? Was it decent you've had one foot in my bed, while in your mind you kept the other in your wife's bed? Was that decent? You entered my body when it's written you were forbidden to even look at my hand. Was that decent? To use me and think you can be accounted a religious man, was that decent or right?

(SARA starts to move off again, PESACH steps in front.)

PESACH: First I loved you, then I made love to you. We did it together. There was no Rezl in our bed, no father-in-law.

(SARA tries to move again, PESACH blocks her.)

SARA: You pretended to love me because I'm useful. A convenient body until your wife got here. I'm what they say in the letters. Harlot, Jezebel, Delilah. It's true, isn't it? Betrayed before. Now for the third time!

PESACH: I don't understand you. A girl who had to punch her way across the Atlantic, who's made a life for herself without the help of family, who's so strong.

SARA: You'll never understand. *(She lunges for his bag.)* I want my ticket. My ticket to Chicago!

(PESACH sidesteps SARA.)

SARA: I'll go there myself. Start a new life without you. I don't need a husband. With all my experience I can be a prostitute in Chicago, and make good money!

PESACH: Stop!!! Stop saying that! Stop.

(PESACH *tries to stop* SARA *from getting hold of the ticket, she punches him, he falls back, mostly out of surprise, pulling her down on top of him, straddling him. He looks up at her, she down at him.)*

SARA: *(Angry, sardonic)* I think I'll go down to the boat with you. I'll meet your wife. I'll tell her what a whore can tell her—that wrapping her legs behind her handsome husband's back has another purpose than the one commanded by God. I'll tell her there is Eden down there! *(She starts to hike up her skirt.)* As there was down here for Pesach!

PESACH: What's happened to you?

SARA: You felt really alive, for the first time, didn't you, the morning after our first time and all our mornings— again and again? It made your morning prayer a truly divine experience! Ask your father in law, right there on the pier "Rabbi, by thrusting my body into the harlot's body— *(Angry copulatory pantomime)* —am I spitting in God's eye!

PESACH: Have you gone crazy?

(PESACH *tries to get up,* SARA *pushes him down.)*

SARA: Whore! Prostitute. Wanton woman. Immoral! That's who I am. Right??

PESACH: No. Shut up! Please shut up.

SARA: Ask the rabbi if his daughter would be so bold as to fornicate with you on in a dark corner of the Fulton Street Ferry, as we did once. No, only the whore will do that!

PESACH: I love you! Don't say those things about us!!

(PESACH *pulls himself up,* SARA *continues shouting. He covers her mouth with his hand. As he holds her, she struggles to free herself.)*

PESACH: Call *me* all the names you want. But not yourself.

(PESACH *continues trying to muzzle her, she escapes.*)

SARA: I shouldn't have stopped Isaac on the boat. I shouldn't have saved myself for you. You're no different than Isaac.

(PESACH *grabs* SARA *again, she frees herself, runs around screaming to the trees and the heavens as he chases after her.*)

SARA: God—listen to me. Pesach is no better than Jews who pray to you three times a day then go out to cheat their neighbors! He prays to you, to seek your blessing while he uses me, he cheats me of my life. I want you to know that about him, God. He used me! Punish him God. He made me into a whore!! His whore.

PESACH: *(Following her)* Shut up! Shut up! Shut up! Shut up!

(PESACH *reaches* SARA, *clumsily tries to restrain her. He crooks his elbow around her head, clamps a hand over her mouth, inadvertently pressuring her neck. We continue to hear her muffled voice. but gradually she is silent, limp. He stares at her, unbelieving. He lays her body on the ground; he tries to waken her, shakes her gently.*)

PESACH: Sara, Sara, wake up. Wake up. *(Kisses her face)* Please! Sara wake up. Wake up. Please. *(Listens to her heart, talks to her and to the heavens alternately)* Sara, sing again. Please sing again. *(Pleading with limp figure)* Sara, this didn't have to be! We would have gone away together. Sara, why couldn't you believe me? *(Turns heavenward)* God, what have I done! Help! Help me! *(Puts her down gently)* Sara, sing again. Please sing again. *(Sad, almost whispered singing)* "Shoo Fly, don't bother me"...Sing!

(Blackout)

Scene Seven

(Fade up slowly, STEPHENSON *emerges to the apron of the stage, spotlighted, addressing the audience as jurors.)*

STEPHENSON: Gentlemen of the Jury, as some of you may have suspected from his sickly appearance in court, and the coughing up of blood we witnessed Pesach Rubenstein died in his cell, this morning. It's the belief of the doctor that Rubenstein passed away from the consumption he contracted earlier in his life. The conditions in the jailhouse probably contributed to the return of this disease, to say nothing of his apparent refusal to eat very much. Whether the Lord took his life or otherwise cannot be known. Pesach Rubenstein emigrated here from a dark corner of Europe. There daily life for centuries was dictated by the many commands of God in the Hebrew bible, bolstered by the close presence of a pious community. Here, I surmise the traditional righteous path was strewn with distraction. I'm told in his dying moments, defendant Rubenstein refused to utter the Hebrew prayer asking God for what we Christians call absolution. I have no idea why. Judge Bell asked me to convey the news of the defendant's passing to you. Asked me too to thank you for serving the cause of justice. The judge's clerk will be out shortly to explain about the voucher you have to sign. *(He walks off.)*

END OF PLAY